WRESTLING SUPERST★RS

SANTINO MARELLA

BY BLAKE MARKEGARD

EPIC

BELLWETHER MEDIA • MINNEAPOLIS, MN

EPIC BOOKS are no ordinary books. They burst with intense action, high-speed heroics, and shadows of the unknown. Are you ready for an Epic adventure?

This edition first published in 2015 by Bellwether Media, Inc.

No part of this publication may be reproduced in whole or in part without written permission of the publisher. For information regarding permission, write to Bellwether Media, Inc., Attention: Permissions Department, 5357 Penn Avenue South, Minneapolis, MN 55419.

Library of Congress Cataloging-in-Publication Data

Markegard, Blake.
  Santino Marella / by Blake Markegard.
    pages cm. – (Epic: Wrestling Superstars)
  Includes bibliographical references and index.
  Summary: "Engaging images accompany information about Santino Marella. The combination of high-interest subject matter and light text is intended for students in grades 2 through 7"– Provided by publisher.
  ISBN 978-1-62617-144-2 (hardcover : alk. paper)
  1. Marella, Santino, 1979–Juvenile literature. 2. Wrestlers–United States–Biography–Juvenile literature. I. Title.
  GV1196.M368M37 2014
  796.812092–dc23
  [B]
                                2014002086

Printed in the United States of America, North Mankato, MN.

TABLE OF CONTENTS

WARNING!

The wrestling moves used in this book are performed by professionals.
Do not attempt to reenact any of the moves performed in this book.

THE DEBUT

Santino Marella watches a WWE event in Milan, Italy. Suddenly, he is pulled from the crowd to wrestle. Umaga waits inside the ring.

UMAGA

Marella is nicknamed The Milan Miracle because of his surprise win.

Umaga beats hard on Marella. But then Bobby Lashley enters the ring. Lashley brings Umaga to the mat. Marella makes the pin. He wins at his debut!

BOBBY LASHLEY

WHO IS SANTINO MARELLA?

MISS SANTINA
★

Santino dressed like a girl
to win Miss WrestleMania
in 2009.

Santino Marella is a showman in the WWE ring. He performs as much as he fights. Sometimes he attacks opponents with a cobra sock puppet.

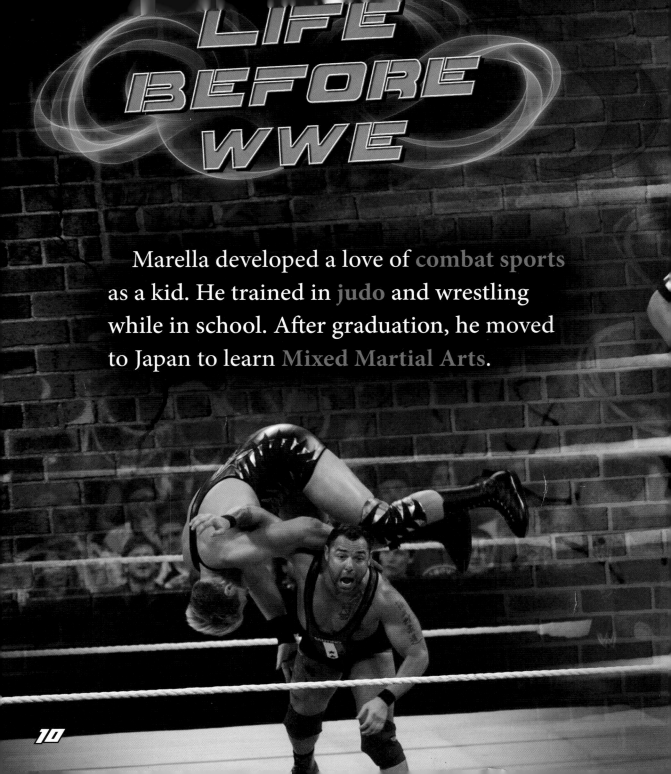

LIFE BEFORE WWE

Marella developed a love of combat sports as a kid. He trained in judo and wrestling while in school. After graduation, he moved to Japan to learn Mixed Martial Arts.

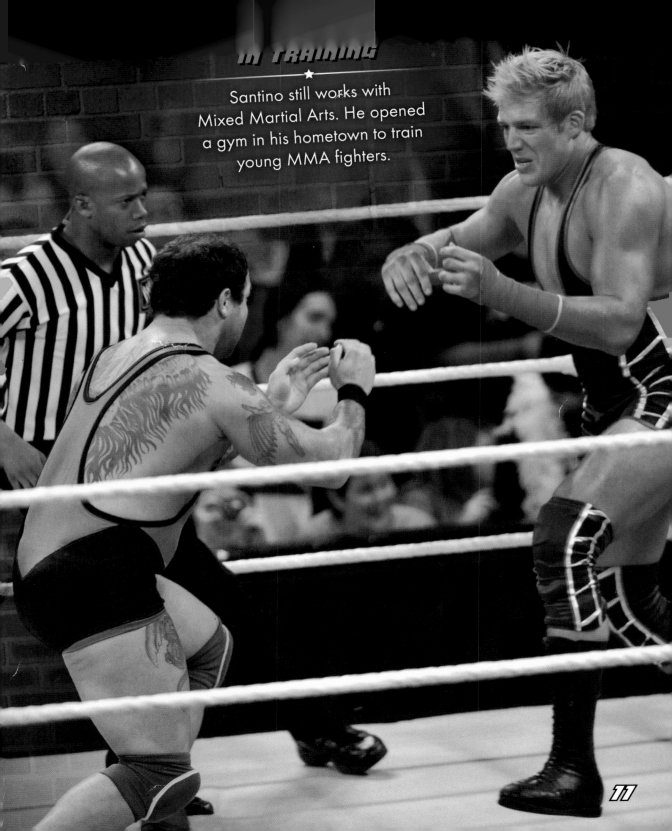

★

Santino still works with
Mixed Martial Arts. He opened
a gym in his hometown to train
young MMA fighters.

Eventually, Marella set his sights on WWE. He started out in developmental leagues in the United States. His ring names were Johnny Geo Basco and Boris Alexiev.

A WWE SUPERSTAR

TWO HOMES

⭐

Marella is actually Canadian. However, he pretends to be from Italy because of his debut.

STAR PROFILE

WRESTLING NAME:	Santino Marella
REAL NAME:	Anthony Carelli
BIRTHDATE:	March 14, 1979
HOMETOWN:	Mississauga, Ontario, Canada
HEIGHT:	6 feet (1.8 meters)
WEIGHT:	233 pounds (106 kilograms)
WWE DEBUT:	2007
FINISHING MOVE:	Cobra Strike

Marella's big break came at his Milan debut.
He was crowned Intercontinental Champion
at the end of his first WWE match.

A second Intercontinental title followed soon after. Later, Marella became United States Champion. The Italian Stallion is driven to become the greatest champion of all time!

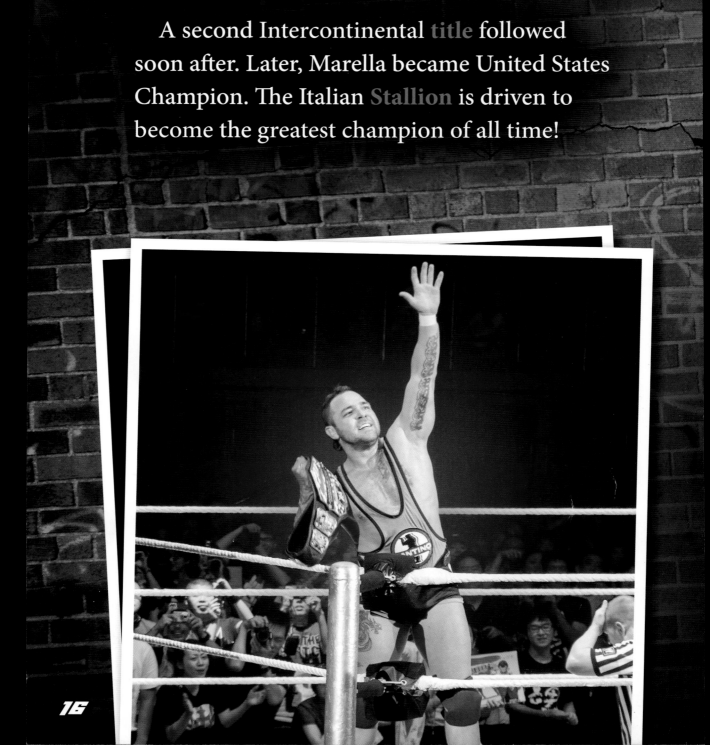

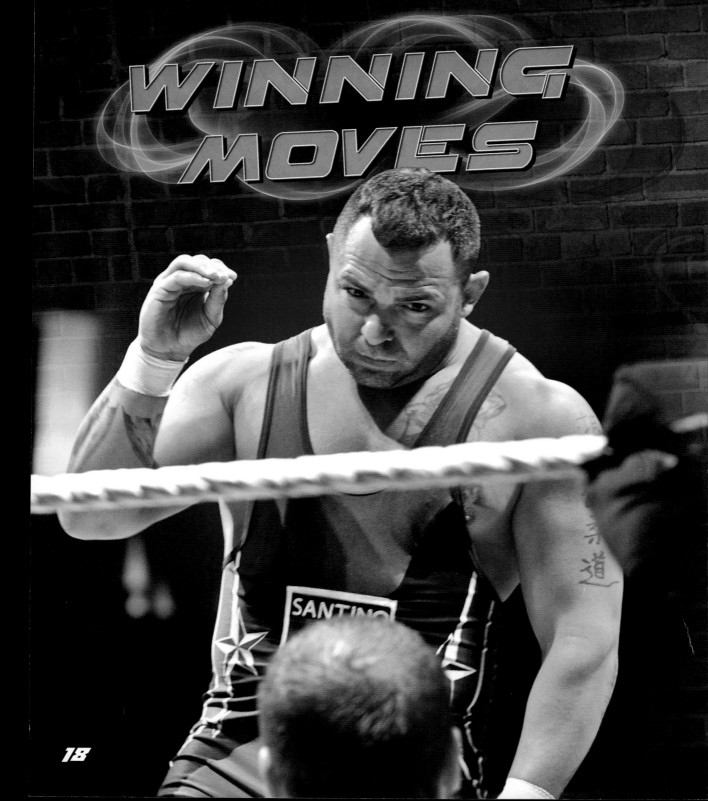

WINNING MOVES

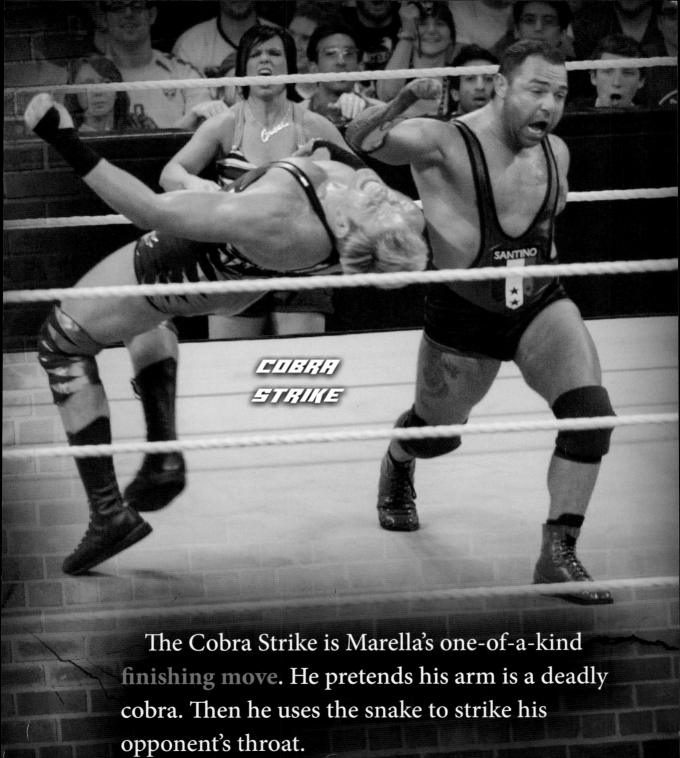

COBRA STRIKE

The Cobra Strike is Marella's one-of-a-kind finishing move. He pretends his arm is a deadly cobra. Then he uses the snake to strike his opponent's throat.

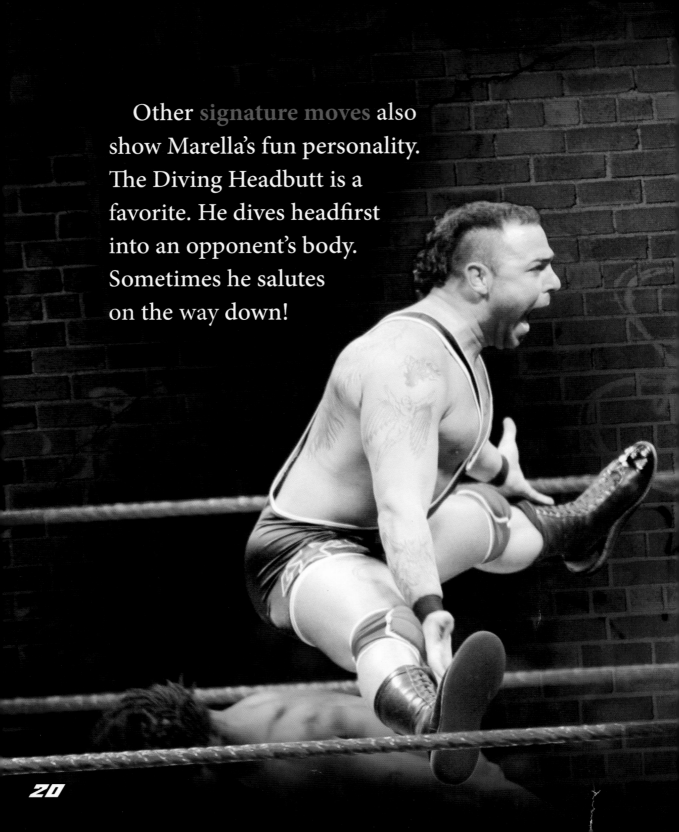

Other signature moves also show Marella's fun personality. The Diving Headbutt is a favorite. He dives headfirst into an opponent's body. Sometimes he salutes on the way down!

DIVING
HEADBUTT

21

GLOSSARY

combat sports—sports in which fighters battle one-on-one

debut—first official appearance

developmental leagues—leagues that allow wrestlers to gain experience and prepare for WWE

finishing move—a wrestling move that finishes off an opponent

intercontinental—involving more than one continent

judo—a Japanese combat sport in which fighters throw or wrestle one another to the ground

Mixed Martial Arts—a combat sport in which fighters use wrestling, boxing, and karate moves

pin—a wrestling hold that ends a match

showman—a person who is an entertaining performer

signature moves—moves that a wrestler is famous for performing

stallion—a male horse used for breeding

title—championship

TO LEARN MORE

At the Library

Black, Jake. *WWE General Manager's Handbook.* New York, N.Y.: Grosset & Dunlap, 2012.

Markegard, Blake. *Rey Mysterio.* Minneapolis, Minn.: Bellwether Media, 2015.

West, Tracey. *Race to the Rumble.* New York, N.Y.: Grosset & Dunlap, 2011.

On the Web

Learning more about Santino Marella is as easy as 1, 2, 3.

1. Go to www.factsurfer.com.

2. Enter "Santino Marella" into the search box.

3. Click the "Surf" button and you will see a list of related web sites.

With factsurfer.com, finding more information is just a click away.

INDEX